OHIO'S GERMAN HERITAGE

Don Heinrich Tolzmann

HERITAGE BOOKS
2011

HERITAGE BOOKS
AN IMPRINT OF HERITAGE BOOKS, INC.

Books, CDs, and more—Worldwide

For our listing of thousands of titles see our website
at
www.HeritageBooks.com

Published 2011 by
HERITAGE BOOKS, INC.
Publishing Division
100 Railroad Ave. #104
Westminster, Maryland 21157

Copyright © 2002 Don Heinrich Tolzmann

All rights reserved. No part of this book may be reproduced or transmitted in any form or by any means, electronic or mechanical, including photocopying, recording or by any information storage and retrieval system without written permission from the author, except for the inclusion of brief quotations in a review.

International Standard Book Numbers
Paperbound: 978-0-7884-2035-1
Clothbound: 978-0-7884-8917-4

TABLE OF CONTENTS

Preface v

1. Introduction 1

2. The Colonial Period 3

3. The New Republic 7

4. Mass Immigration and Settlement 11

5. The World Wars Period 17

6. The Roots and Ethnic Revival Period 21

7. Resources 23

8. Conclusion 25

Select Bibliography 27

Index 31

PREFACE

The following account is the forerunner of a more comprehensive history of the German element in Ohio, which the author plans to complete in the future. In the meantime, this work is presented to provide an introduction to Ohio's German heritage. I was motivated to bring out this introductory survey, as Ohio's Bicentennial will soon be celebrated, and it appeared to be more than appropriate to contribute to this event by making this work available at this time. With this brief survey, I have aimed to trace the basic outlines of German immigration and settlement in the history of the state. Those interested in further reading on the topic are referred to the select bibliography.

Don Heinrich Tolzmann
University of Cincinnati

1. INTRODUCTION

Ohio is a state consisting of 41,000 square miles, and is 210 by 225 miles in width and length, which today has a population of roughly 11 million. As a result of the U. S. Census we know that 40% of the state's population claim German ancestry, or roughly 4 ½ million. Today, Ohio's German-American element represents the third largest concentration in actual numbers of German-Americans in the U. S., following California and Pennsylvania, respectively. In speaking of Ohio's German heritage, we may well ask the question of how Ohio came by its large German element.

As the largest ethnic element in the state, German-Americans have exerted, and not surprisingly given their statistics, a profound influence on all aspects of life in the history of the state. Located in all 88 counties, German-Americans are in the clear majority in 61 of them. German-American history is, hence, not only an important aspect of Ohio history, it is to a great extent Ohio history, which is to say that one cannot speak of Ohio history without reference to 40% of the state's population.

Again, with regard to the U. S. Census, it has been observed that the most striking feature about Ohio is the strong concentration of the German element. The purpose of this essay is to provide an introductory history to Ohio's German heritage, as well as to address the seemingly paradoxical question of how the history of Ohio's major ethnic group has remained relatively obscure until the recent past.

From this vantage point, we may, therefore, look backwards to trace how this came to be. Five basic periods in Ohio German history can be identified: 1. The Colonial Period (before the American Revolution); 2. The New Republic (until 1830); 3. The Mass Migration and Settlement Period (from 1830 to World War I); 4. The

World Wars Period; and 5. The Roots and Ethnic Revival Period of the latter half of the 20th century and beyond.

2. THE COLONIAL PERIOD

In the Colonial period, Ohio became the pawn at center stage in the international conflict between France and England. The French first came to the region in the 17th century, when the explorer, LaSalle, claimed the Ohio and Mississippi Valleys for the king of France. It should be noted that the extent of French penetration of the frontier was extensive, and it should be remembered that New France, or Quebec, was located to the north, and that French frontier forts and trading posts could be found in Michigan.

Given this extensive network of frontier trading posts, it is not surprising that other trappers and traders came to Ohio. And the first German we find in Ohio came in 1728 when Anton Sodowsky established a trading post on the banks of Lake Erie. Today, the city of Sandusky bears his name. This is the beginning date in Ohio German history. In 1740, two Virginia Germans (Thomas Morlin and Johann Salling) came on a trading tour through the Ohio territory, and exchanged goods for furs with the Native Americans.

At this point, it is well to take note of the geographical location of Ohio: It was located directly west of the major settlement areas of the colonial German element. To the east was Pennsylvania, which was already 1/3 German. South of Pennsylvania was Maryland and the Virginias, which also had substantial German elements. Hence, by the 1740s German-Americans had already established a trading post and had been engaged in trading tours in the Ohio territory.

In 1750, the Ohio Land company was established in Virginia, and Christoph Gist (Geist), a Maryland German, was charged to explore the western territory. He became the first European American to explore Ohio extensively and with care, and it should be noted that he preceded Daniel Boone by eighteen years. It should also be noted that when Boone came through the Ohio Valley on his way to Kentucky, that German-Americans were with him, since he himself came from a Pennsylvania German settlement, and spoke the Pennsylvania German dialect, although he himself was not German. In the meantime, war was on the horizon, and in 1756 the French and Indian War broke out. Both France and England claimed Ohio as their territory. The governor of Virginia had dispatched George Washington and Gist to Ohio to warn the French that they were on land claimed by the English colony of Virginia. The English victory in 1763 resulted in England taking control not only of the Ohio Valley, but also of Canada. In this and the following frontier wars, the Native Americans sided mainly with the French, rather than the English, and the period from the end of the French and Indian War down to the American Revolution in 1776 was marked by continual frontier warfare. From 1763 to 1765, there occurred Pontiac's War, and in 1774 Lord Dunsmore's War took place in which the governor of Virginia sent an expedition to defeat the Indians and press Virginia's claims. In this context of frontier warfare, the first settlements of colonial America were established in Ohio.

It was in the 1760s and 1770s that we see the first settlements being established by German-Americans. In 1761, the first European American settler in Ohio history, Christian Friedrich Post, came to what is now Stark County, Ohio, and there erected the first frontier dwelling in Ohio. He was a German Moravian who had come from Bethlehem, Pennsylvania, and he represents the early wave of Pennsylvania German settlement into Ohio.

The outlook of the German Moravians with regard to the Indians was quite different from that of Anglo-Americans, who were establishing the frontier policy of manifest destiny. Here they sowed the seeds of the policy which became one of expulsion. This can be contrasted sharply to that of the French who lived with and intermarried with the Indians. The German Moravian Post himself married an Ohio Indian, and the Moravians established missions which seriously attempted to create a new model for communication and cooperation with the Native Americans.

The Moravians not only learned the Indian languages, but compiled the first grammars and dictionaries of these languages. They became bilingual, as did the Indians they worked with in Ohio. At their settlements, German, English, and the Indian languages were spoken. Because of this different orientation towards the Ohio Indians, the Anglo-Americans on the frontier had grave misgivings and mistrust towards the German Moravians, which would result in frontier tragedy, and the eventual destruction of the German Moravian settlements.

In 1772, the first actual frontier settlement was established in the Tuscarawas Valley in northeast Ohio by the well known German Moravian missionary, David Zeisberger. The settlement was known as Schoenbrunn (German for beautiful spring/creek). Other settlements soon followed in the area: Gnadenhuetten (German for huts of grace), Lichtenau (German for the meadow of light), and Salem.

The first recorded births of European Americans in Ohio occurred at these first settlements: in 1773, the first male was born, Johann Roth, and in 1782, the first female, Johanna Heckewelder. At Schoenbrunn, the first church building and school house in Ohio were erected. It was Zeisberger who translated several books from German into the Indian languages, and wrote an Indian grammar which was published in Philadelphia. By 1775, the number of Indians in his congregations numbered 415, most of whom could understand some German.

As a result of the American Revolution, the British and their Indian allies engaged in warfare against the Americans on the Ohio frontier. A particular sore point to them were the German Moravian settlements, which were plundered in 1781. In the meantime, many Americans on the frontier felt that the British were in alliance with the Indians, and again adopted an anti-Indian policy. In their view, there was no difference between the British Indian allies and the Christian Indians at the German Moravian settlements. As a result of this misperception, an expedition of settlers from Pittsburgh attacked Gnadenhuetten in 1782, and killed 62 adults and 34 children in one of the most tragic of frontier history. At nearby Schoenbrunn, the inhabitants barely escaped the frontier attackers, who after their return to Pittsburgh were viewed dividedly as either heroes or murderers, which is an indication of the moral ambivalence of American frontier history.

Had the German Moravian Indian philosophy been allowed to stand, then perhaps there would have been a different history of the American frontier—at least, this is what German-American historians have maintained in their histories in the past.

3. THE NEW REPUBLIC

After the American Revolution, the first major German immigration into Ohio continued into the area originally settled by the Moravians, and extended westwards across Ohio into what became known as the Backbone Counties of Ohio. The names of the settlements they established reflect whether they were of sectarian background or not. Places with Biblical names, such as Bethlehem, Salem, Nazareth, Goshen, and Canaan, were established by sectarian groups, whereas non-sectarians established places such as New Lancaster and Germantown, named for German-American settlements in Pennsylvania. Also, they named places for heroes of the Revolution, such as Steubenville. The sectarian settlements, especially those established by the Amish and the Mennonites, remain today as some of the major concentrations of these early German-American settlers.

A Pennsylvania German named Ebenezer Zahn in 1796 established what became known as Zane's Trace, a path from Wheeling, West Virginia to Maysville, Kentucky on the Ohio River. Along this path, many Pennsylvania, Maryland, and Virginia Germans came and then boarded keelboats on the Ohio River, and then settled at various points along the Ohio, especially at Cincinnati. Zahn's granddaughter, it may be noted, named her son Zane Grey after her illustrious grandfather. He wrote numerous books about the frontier and wild west. In 1906, he published one which dealt specifically with the Ohio frontier, *The Spirit of the Border*, which he described as "a tale of high courage of our forefathers who hewed an empire out of the trackless wild."

Zane's Trace (Anglo-Americans could not pronounce the German name "Zahn" and hence said "Zane"), brings into focus the second major early area of German settlement - along the Ohio River.

Germans always preferred settling along water and riverways. In the north, they moved westward, staying close to the Great Lakes, and in the south, they followed the Ohio River, thus resulting in concentrations of German settlements in these areas.

In 1788, when Cincinnati was founded, there were a few Germans amongst the first settlers. In 1792, the first written report about Cincinnati and other Ohio settlements was recorded by the German Moravian missionary, Johann Heckewelder, who before the Revolution had been with Zeisberger in northeastern Ohio. By the 1790s, many Germans were coming down the Ohio River. Among the early settlers was Christian Waldschmidt who in 1795/96 established Deutschland, which became known as Germany, the first German settlement in southwestern Ohio; today the Waldschmidt House, located in northeastern Cincinnati, is a historic site maintained by the Daughters of the American Revolution. Here the first mills were established in Ohio, which produced the first paper in the area which was used for books and newspapers.

In 1807, *Der Ohio Adler*, Ohio's first German-language newspaper, was published at New Lancaster. In the same year, an almanac was published in Cincinnati, *Teutscher Calender auf 1808*, which like the newspaper was in the Pennsylvania German dialect, another indication of the preponderance of the Pennsylvania Germans at the time. This is an important point when studying early Ohio German history, since it is often concluded that there were few Germans in Ohio in these early years, when in actuality there were numerous German-speaking Americans.

One must pay close attention to all those who are from Pennsylvania, Maryland, and Virginia, since in many cases one will find that they are German surnamed, and part of this early wave of settlement by colonial German-Americans. It should be noted that the ancestral homeland in Europe of these German-Americans was in the southwestern German-speaking realm, which encompassed the Palatinate, Baden, Wuerttemberg, Alsace-Lorraine, and Switzerland.

One American-born Maryland German, Martin Baum, came to cincinnati in 1795, and it was he who established Cincinnati as a city with a reputation as a destination for German immigrants. His parents came from the Alsace, and had left because of the continual French incursions into German territory. Baum established numerous businesses, including a bank, sugar refinery, and an iron foundry in Cincinnati. To attract workers for his various enterprises, he sent agents to the port cities of New Orleans, New York, Philadelphia, and Baltimore, where they recruited recently arrived German immigrants. This established Cincinnati with a reputation as a place where German immigrants could find employment, a reputation which continued even long after the days of Baum.

Germans were not only coming individually and with their families, there were also a number of settlement societies which formed colonies in Ohio. In 1817, the communitarian settlement of Zoar was established by Josef Baeumler and others from Wuerttemberg. Another communitarian settlement, located near Canton, was Teutonia, which was founded by Peter Kaufmann in 1826. He had briefly been a member of the communitarian settlement of Economy, Pennsylvania, located near Pittsburgh, which by the 1820s was becoming a major settlement and distribution center for recently arrived German immigrants.

Pittsburgh was also located at the mouth of the Ohio River, and from here immigrants boarded boats on the Ohio River, and traveled west. They also moved straight into Ohio by means of the extensive network of roads which by now had replaced Zane's Trace. By 1817, the German element of Ohio was so substantial that the state legislature decided to authorize the printing of the state laws and constitution in German; not until 1828 would such a motion be submitted in the Pennsylvania legislature, which is an indication of the early strong impact of German settlement in Ohio

The German immigration since the Revolution had been predominantly German-American from Pennsylvania, Maryland, and Virginia, but by the close of the Napoleonic wars, the European German immigration began to increase. Germans headed to the port cities, and from these ports, they traveled to Pittsburgh, or to points along the Ohio River–from these locations they could move directly into Ohio, or take the river further west. From New Orleans, they would take the Mississippi north, and then the Ohio River east to Ohio.

4. MASS IMMIGRATION AND SETTLEMENT

In this period, we see the mass immigration from the German-speaking states of Europe. Place-names established in this period reflect the European immigration, such as: Berlin, Wirtemberg, Saxon, Hanover, Dresden, Osnaburg, Frankfurt, Spires, Potsdam, Winesburg, Strasburg, New Bremen, Minster, etc. This period saw several waves of immigration. In the 1830s, the Thirtyers came, which consisted of refugees of the revolutions of that decade. Although small in number, this group included intellectuals, doctors, lawyers, professors, journalists etc., and it was they who established high quality German-American newspapers across the state, such as the *Cincinnati Volksblatt*, founded in 1836.

The next major wave were the Forty-Eighters, the name given to all those who came after the failed revolution of 1848. Although only a few thousand were actually involved in the revolution, thousands more came who were discontented with the social, political, and economical situation in the German states.

In the 1870s, Bismarck led his Kulturkampf against the Catholic Church, thus causing a sizable immigration of German Catholics to America, and in the 1880s he maintained an anti-socialist policy by means of legislation against the socialists, thus causing numerous German Social Democrats, including members of the Reichstag, to immigrate. Aside from these very perceptible groups, there was massive immigration to America for economic reasons. The U. S. was still viewed at the land of "unlimited possibilities."

It is in this period we see the foundation of all the institutions and ways of life which we readily identify as "German-American." In 1840, the first public bilingual school system in the U. S. was established in Cincinnati, and soon spread across the state. All of the religious denominations, of course, established their own German-language parochial school systems. In 1844, German-Americans from Cincinnati elected Charles Ruemelin to the state legislature to represent German-American interests at the state level; he was a refugee of the revolution of the 1830s. In 1871, the Ohio Germans helped elect a Forty-Eighter from Cleveland, Jakob Mueller, as Lieutenant Governor of the state. Hence, from the 1840s to the 1870s, German-Americans were taking an active role in state politics.

By 1850, the state population was about 2 million, and the German element was moving close to what it is today in terms of percentage. The German immigration in the years since the Napoleonic wars was staggeringly dramatic. In Cincinnati, for example, the population in 1820 was ca. 5% German, but by 1850 it was 30%. The German immigration of these years established what was called "ethnic Americanization." Yes, immigrants would become Americans, but that meant becoming a citizen, it had nothing to do whatsoever with one's ethnic background. Ethnic Americanization meant that one would become an ethnic American. For Germans, this meant one was no longer a German, but rather a German-American. Americanization, therefore, did not mean Anglicization.

German-Americans were proud to be American citizens, but they wanted to maintain their own heritage, and this they did by establishing German-language institutions; newspapers, churches, societies, etc. In many communities, the only newspaper was German, as were all the other institutions and businesses. German-Americans also founded institutions of higher learning. There is, for example, the German Methodist College, Baldwin-Wallace College at Berea, the German Lutheran Capital University in Columbus, the German Lutheran Wittenberg University in Springfield, among others. Clearly, German-Americans were interested in maintaining their German heritage.

In the previous period, German-Americans had established settlements along the Ohio River and in northern Ohio. In this period, when Cincinnati becomes a major destination point of German immigrants, we see them landing at Cincinnati and then moving northwards, which resulted in the western portions of the state forming a German settlement corridor all the way to Lake Erie. Indeed, many German immigrants obtained employment working on the Miami-Erie Canal, which was built from 1825-40. The immigrants in this part of Ohio came mainly from northwestern Germany, and hence, the names Bremen and Minster can be found there, and the Low German dialect is still spoken and understood there.

This northern settlement movement in western Ohio crossed paths in northwestern Ohio with the older Pennsylvania German settlement movement. This older Pennsylvania German settlement region moved westwards, and extended over into northeastern Indiana. Cincinnati, after 1830, became the major distribution point for the German immigration in the Midwest, and remained so until the Civil War, after which it was replaced by other western cities, such as St. Louis, and Milwaukee, but continued to remain a major German-American center. Together with Milwaukee and St. Louis it formed what became known as the "German Triangle" because of the concentration of the German immigration in this region. Other German-American centers in Ohio were in the urban areas, including Columbus, Cleveland, Toledo, etc., and as noted earlier, the rural areas became predominantly German (2/3 of the counties).

As Ohio became a state with a strong German heritage in what was known as the Midwestern German Belt (states extending from Pennsylvania all the way to the west coast), Germans profoundly affected the whole way of life. This was particularly evident in the German-American reaction to the institution of slavery. German-

Americans were shocked that in a country they had believed was a citadel of democracy that human beings were being held in bondage. In the election of 1860, there is no question that the German vote throughout the Midwest held the balance of power and the election returns clearly demonstrate that the Midwest went with the cause of Abraham Lincoln. When it came to the Civil War, German-Americans from Ohio formed eleven regiments; it also should be noted that 1/4 of the Union Army consisted of German-Americans.

As a result of the political developments of the 1850s/60s, German-Americans had joined the Republican Party in large numbers. After the Civil War, when the Republicans of Ohio wanted to obtain advice on issues pertaining to state political reform, they invited Carl Schurz in 1871. He then came and toured the state, and addressed the state legislature in the methodology of reform. Again, this was an indication of the stature and high regard in which the German element was held. At this time, German-Americans felt special pride in having fought for the Union, and also were proud of the fact that their ancestral homeland had been successfully united as the German Empire.

In 1883, the German-American Bicentennial was widely celebrated across the state of Ohio, and commemorated the founding in 1683 of the first permanent German settlement in America at Germantown, Pennsylvania. In the years thereafter, numerous societies were formed in rural and urban areas to celebrate the date Germantown was founded, the 6th of October. This evolved into the idea of celebrating this date annually as "German Day," and the first such day in Ohio was held in Cleveland in 1890, and then in 1895 in Cincinnati, and elsewhere thereafter.

By 1902, German-American societies from across Ohio met in Cleveland, and formed the German-American Alliance of Ohio, which was the state branch of the National German-American

Alliance, which was headquartered in Philadelphia. In 1907, the Ohio Alliance sponsored its first statewide celebration of German Day in Toledo on 6 October. In 1910, President Taft who was from Cincinnati, dedicated the Steuben Monument, located in front of the White House, and praised not only Baron von Steuben, but German-Americans in general for their contributions to the building of the nation. At this time, there were fifty-eight newspapers being published in German in Ohio: 6 daily, 44 weekly, and 8 monthly publications. The major German-American newspapers were the *Volksblatt* and the *Freie Presse* in Cincinnati; the *Waechter und Anzeiger* in Cleveland; the *Volkszeitung* in Dayton; the *Express und Westbote* in Columbus; and the *Express* in Toledo. All seemed well until the advent of the First World War.

5. THE WORLD WARS PERIOD

When war broke out in 1914, German-Americans had not been closely following European affairs. Indeed, their main political interest and concern at the time was opposing all attempts to establish a state law mandating prohibition. However, when war did break out, they were naturally as pro-German, as Anglo-Americans were pro-British. A large number of German-Americans who had come from Austro-Hungary were also in favor of their ancestral homeland; most of the latter were in the urban areas, such as Cincinnati, Cleveland, Toledo, and Columbus.

Wilson's request for a declaration of war against Germany set loose an anti-German hysteria which had tragic repercussion in a state such as Ohio with its large German element. The crimes and wrongs committed against German-Americans during the First World War are well documented by Carl Wittke, and it would be beyond the scope of this essay to discuss the anti-German hysteria. There were attempted lynchings, tarrings and featherings, book burnings, mobs, ethnic harassment and intimidation.

The world war also resulted in the breakup of the German and the Austrian Empires, thus resulting in more immigration to America, and to Ohio. Especially now came many from the former provinces of the old Austrian Empire, and in the 1920s the disastrous inflation in Germany caused more to come.

The 1920s were difficult years for the German element since they witnessed what German-Americans considered as a continuation of war-engendered nativism. In 1919, the Governor of Ohio had procured from the state the kind of legislation which banned German instruction below the 8th grade in public, private, and parochial schools. Not until 1923 was this law declared unconstitutional; it had been brought as a test case by Missouri Synod German-American

Lutherans from Cleveland, and the case was defended by Charles Hogan, former Ohio Attorney General who was well known as an Irish-American leader in Ohio. Another law of concern was the Volstead Act which mandated national prohibition, and which stood in place until 1933. German-Americans considered this an anti-German piece of legislation, since most brewers and brewery workers were German-American. It also had an adverse impact on the German-American press since it had been the major source of advertising income. It also had an adverse impact on German-American social life - try to imagine an Oktoberfest without the brew.

If 1933 brought with it good news regarding the downfall of prohibition, it also meant trouble on the horizon with the National Socialist seizure of power in Germany. Indeed, the Third Reich would cause more to immigrate, including German Jews and intellectuals opposed to the regime. The end of the war caused another massive wave of immigration, especially as a result of the expulsion of millions, such as the Danube Swabians, from their homelands in eastern and southeastern Europe. This postwar immigration was further augmented by G.I. war brides, so that by the 1950s there was the last great wave of immigration, which would only taper off by 1970, when it greatly declines, especially due to the economic recovery in Europe.

Aside from providing an introduction to Ohio's German heritage, this essay also aims to address the question of how the history and heritage of Ohio's major ethnic group has remained relatively obscure until the recent past. The major reason that the German-Americans of Ohio have not been accorded the historical recognition due to them is because of the anti-German hostilities engendered by the world wars. During and after these wars, German-Americans were no longer judged by their contributions to their communities and American society, but were judged by external events in Europe. Aside from the wartime ordeal, which included the almost completely unknown internment of German-Americans, many were stigmatized and stereotyped for no other reason than that they were of German descent. Their historical record was generally belittled, distorted, or ignored. It took many years to recover from their status of wartime pariahs. Not until the ethnic revival of the 1970s was there again wide scale public recognition and pride in the German heritage.

6. THE ROOTS AND ETHNIC REVIVAL PERIOD

In the postwar era, German-Americans began actively repairing the damage done by the war. By the 1950s German Day celebrations were again being held across Ohio, and in 1958 the 275th anniversary of the founding of Germantown was celebrated. In 1968, the Society for German-American Studies was established by Robert E. Ward at Youngstown State University, and it became the major single society for those interested in German-American Studies.

Especially beneficial to German-Americans was the occurrence in 1970 of the roots/ethnic revival phenomenon. Nationally, there was interest in one's roots, family history, and ethnic background. This became know also as the new ethnicity, as American society finally came to the awareness and acceptance that it was not a melting pot, but rather a culturally diverse nation, or as President Kennedy stated, a nation of nations.

In 1976, the American Bicentennial was celebrated, and increasing attention was placed on the role German-Americans had played in the building of the nation and the state. German-American societies participated in numerous Bicentennial activities, and conferences, exhibits, and symposia were held at various colleges and universities which focused on the German heritage.

Then in 1983, the Tricentennial of the founding of Germantown was celebrated. For the celebration, Gov. Celeste appointed a special German-American Tricentennial Commission. This was the first formal recognition of Ohio's German heritage since before the world wars, and symbolized the return of German-Americans to active involvement in the affairs of the state, as well as the renewed pride in the German heritage.

In 1987, the Society for German-American Studies led a national campaign which resulted in the national proclamation by President

Reagan of the 6th of October as German-American Day. The Ohio German Heritage council, the successor to the 1983 state Tricentennial Commission, obtained state proclamations from Gov. Voinovich declaring October as German-American Heritage Month, beginning in 1991, and state proclamations have also been issued annually by Gov. Taft. In 1992, the Ohio Historical Society endorsed the celebration of October as German-American Heritage Month also, as did the Ohio foreign Language Association. By the 21st century, German-American Day and Month were celebrated and acknowledged across Ohio.

7. RESOURCES

1. Libraries and Archives:

Those interested in researching Ohio's German heritage should consult the Ohio Historical Society, the many local and county historical societies, and the libraries of archives of colleges and universities. Also, special reference should be made to the German-Americana Collection at the University of Cincinnati. A two volume catalog of this collection has been published, and should be consulted by anyone interested in Ohio's German heritage. See the selective bibliography for further information. Also, reference should be made to the German-American Genealogical Library in Columbus, the Palatines to America National Library

2. The Press:

In the state of Ohio over 500 German-language newspapers and periodicals have been published, which provide historical and biographical information obtainable nowhere else. Today, the major German-language newspaper in Ohio is the *Germania*, published in Cleveland. Also, the *Nordamerikanische Wochenpost*, published in Detroit, carries news from and about Ohio, as does the *Amerika Woche* from Chicago, and the *Staats-Zeitung* from New York. Among the special interest publications is *Der Nord-Amerikanische Calender*, published by the Amish in Baltic, Ohio. Also, the number of newsletters published by German-American societies in Ohio numbers well over a hundred.

3. Secular and Religious

Organizations and Institutions: there are today over 100 German-American societies across the state, some of them dating back as far as 1848 (Cincinnati Turner Society). Many of them maintain records with valuable membership information, as well as historical documents. The religious institutions (churches, seminaries, colleges and universities), of course, maintain a wealth of material on German-Americans belonging to particular denominations, e.g. the German Methodist Collection at Baldwin-Wallace College.

4. German instruction:

Instruction in German is available at 44 colleges and universities across Ohio, and at numerous high schools. At the elementary level it is also available at a number of schools; including private parochial, and public schools.

8. CONCLUSION

Clearly, The German dimension has played a major role in the history of the state of Ohio. Indeed, no history of the state is complete which does not include treatment of such a major segment of the population (40%). Unfortunately, many local and regional histories provide little, or no mention of the German heritage. As noted above, this was due to the adverse impact of the period of the world wars. It has only been since the 1970s that serious research has begun in the field of German-American Studies. For these reasons the challenge is great to tell the story of Ohio's major ethnic element, and the important role it has played in building of the state since the 18th century.

SELECT BIBLIOGRAPHY

1. Bibliographic Guides:

Bibliographic references to works dealing with the history of German immigration, settlement, and influences in Ohio can be found in the following works of the author: *German-Americana: A Bibliography*. (Metuchen, NJ: Scarecrow Press, 1975), and *Catalog of the German-Americana Collection, University of Cincinnati*. (Muenchen: K. G. Saur, 1990). Both of these works should be consulted to locate some of the older publications, especially those published in the German language. A bibliography of the German-American newspapers published in Ohio can be found in: Karl J. Arndt, *The German Language Press of the Americas*. (Muenchen: Verlag Dokumentation, 1976).

2. Regional and Specialized Works:

Becker, Carl. *The Village, A History of Germantown, Ohio, 1804-1976*. (Germantown, Ohio: Germantown Historical Society, 1980).

Kaufman, Stanley. *Germanic Folk Culture in Eastern Ohio*. (Walnut Creek, Ohio: German Culture Museum, 1986).

Kaufmann, Wilhelm. *The Germans in the American Civil War: With a Biographical Directory.* Translated by Steven Rowan and edited by Don Heinrich Tolzmann with Werner D. Mueller and Robert E. Ward. (Carlisle, PA: John Kallmann, 1999).

Klauprecht, Emil. *German Chronicle in the History of the Ohio Valley, and its Capital Cincinnati, Cincinnati, in Particular.*

Translated by Dale V. Lally and edited by Don Heinrich Tolzmann. (Bowie, MD: Heritage Books, Inc., 1992).

Morhart, Hilda Dischinger. *The Zoar Story*. (Dover, Ohio: Siebert Printing Col, 1968).

Ott, Franziska C. *Cincinnati German Imprints*. (Columbus, Ohio: The Columbus Maennerchor, 1968).

Rowan, Steven, ed., *Cleveland and its Germans*. (Cleveland: Western Reserve Historical Society, 1998).

Schreiber, William. *Our Amish Neighbors*. (Chicago: University of Chicago Press, 1962).

Thode, Ernest. *Germans Into and Out of Ohio Before 1850*, (Columbus, Ohio: Ohio Chapter Palatines to America, 1993).

_____, *The Jubilee Edition of the Cleveland Waechter und Anzeiger, 1902*. (Cleveland: Western Reserve Historical Society, 2000).

Tolzmann, Don Heinrich. *Cincinnati's German Heritage*. (Bowie, MD: Heritage Books, Inc., 1994).

_____. *Dayton's German Heritage: Karl Karstaedt's Jubilee History of the German Pioneer society of Dayton, Ohio*. (Bowie, MD: Heritage Books, Inc., 2001).

_____. *The Ohio Valley German Biographical Index*. (Bowie, MD: Heritage Books, Inc., 1992), and *Supplement*. (1993).

_____. *Das Ohiotal–The Ohio Valley: The German Dimension.* (New York: Peter Lang Pub. Co., 1992).

Ward, Robert E. *An Annotated Bibliography of Materials Pertaining to the German-speaking Immigrants of Greater Cleveland and the Communities of Northern Ohio.* (Parma, Ohio: Society for German-American Studies, 1974).

_____. *German Day in Greater Cleveland: June 4, 1989.* (Cleveland: HB Laser Communications, 1989).

3. Websites:

German-American Studies at the University of Cincinnati
    http://www.artsci.uc.edu/german/geram.htm

German-Americana Collection, University of Cincinnati
    http://www.archives.uc.edu/german

German Heritage Museum
    http://www.gacl.org/museum.html

Library- Palatines to America
    wysiwyg://113/http://genealogy.org/~palm/library.htm

INDEX

Arndt, Karl J. 27
Baeumler, Josef 9
Baum, Martin 9
Becker, Carl 27
Bismarck 11
Boone, Daniel 3
Celeste, Gov. 21
Dunsmore, Lord 4
Geist, Christoph 3
Gist, Christoph 3, 4
Heckewelder, Johann 8
Heckewelder, Johanna 5
Hogan, Charles 18
Kaufman, Stanley 27
Kaufmann, Peter 9
Kaufmann, Wilhelm 27
Kennedy, President 21
Klauprecht, Emil 27
Lally, Dale 28
LaSalle 3
Lincoln, Abraham 14
Morhart, Hilda Dischinger 28
Morlin, Thomas 3
Mueller, Jakob 12
Mueller, Werner 27
Ott, Franziska C. 28
Pontiac 4
Post, Christian Friedrich 4
Reagan, President 22

Roth, Johann ... 5
Rowan, Steven ... 28
Salling, Johann ... 3
Schreiber, William ... 28
Schurz, Carl ... 14
Sodowsky, Anton ... 3
Taft, Gov. ... 22
Taft, President ... 15
Thode, Ernest ... 28
Tolzmann, Don Heinrich ... 27, 28
Voinovich, Gov. ... 22
Waldschmidt, Christian ... 8
Ward, Robert E. ... 21, 27, 29
Washington, George ... 4
Wittke, Carl ... 17
Zahn, Ebenezer ... 7
Zeisberger, David ... 5, 8

Other Heritage Books by Don Heinrich Tolzmann:

Amana: William Rufus Perkins' and Barthinius L. Wick's History of the Amana Society, or Community of True Inspiration

Americana Germanica: Paul Ben Baginsky's Bibliography of German Works Relating to America, 1493–1800

Biography of Baron Von Steuben, the Army of the American Revolution and Its Organizer: Rudolf Cronau's Biography of Baron von Steuben

CD: *German-American Biographical Index (Midwest Families)*

CD: *Germans, Volume 2*

CD: *The German Colonial Era* (four volumes)

Cincinnati's German Heritage

Covington's German Heritage

Custer: Frederick Whittaker's Complete Life of General George A. Custer, Major General of Volunteers, Brevet Major General U.S. Army and Lieutenant-Colonel Seventh U.S. Cavalry

Dayton's German Heritage: Karl Karstaedt's Golden Jubilee History of the German Pioneer Society of Dayton, Ohio

Early German-American Newspapers: Daniel Miller's History

German Americans in the Revolution

German Immigration to America: The First Wave

German Pioneer Life and Domestic Customs

German Pioneer Lifestyle

German Pioneers in Early California: Erwin G. Gudde's History

German-American Achievements: 400 Years of Contributions to America

German-Americana: A Bibliography

Germany and America, 1450–1700

Kentucky's German Pioneers: H. A. Rattermann's History

Lives and Exploits of the Daring Frank and Jesse James: Thaddeus Thorndike's Graphic and Realistic Description of Their Many Deeds of Unparalleled Daring in the Robbing of Banks and Railroad Trains

Louisiana's German Heritage: Louis Voss' Introductory History

Maryland's German Heritage: Daniel Wunderlich Nead's History

Memories of the Battle of New Ulm: Personal Accounts of the Sioux Uprising. L. A. Fritsche's History of Brown County, Minnesota (1916)

Michigan's German Heritage: John Andrew Russell's History of the German Influence in the Making of Michigan

Ohio's German Heritage

Outbreak and Massacre by the Dakota Indians in Minnesota in 1862: Marion P. Satterlee's Minute Account of the Outbreak, with Exact Locations, Names of All Victims, Prisoners at Camp Release, Refugees at Fort Ridgely, etc. Complete List of Indians Killed in Battle and Those Hung, and Those Pardoned at Rock Island, Iowa

The German Element in Virginia: Herrmann Schuricht's History

The German Immigrant in America

The Pennsylvania Germans: James Owen Knauss, Jr.'s Social History

The Pennsylvania Germans: Jesse Leonard Rosenberger's Sketch of Their History and Life

www.ingramcontent.com/pod-product-compliance
Lightning Source LLC
Chambersburg PA
CBHW061518040426
42450CB00008B/1674